MONSTERS!

WITCHES

PETER CASTELLANO

Gareth Stevens
PUBLISHING

Please visit our website, www.garethstevens.com. For a free color catalog of all our high-quality books, call toll free 1-800-542-2595 or fax 1-877-542-2596.

Library of Congress Cataloging-in-Publication Data

Castellano, Peter.
Witches / Peter Castellano.
    pages cm. — (Monsters!)
Includes index.
ISBN 978-1-4824-4102-4 (pbk.)
ISBN 978-1-4824-4103-1 (6 pack)
ISBN 978-1-4824-4104-8 (library binding)
1. Witches—Juvenile literature. I. Title.
BF1566.C325 2016
133.4'3—dc23

2015034677

First Edition

Published in 2016 by
Gareth Stevens Publishing
111 East 14th Street, Suite 349
New York, NY 10003

Copyright © 2016 Gareth Stevens Publishing

Designer: Samantha DeMartin
Editor: Kristen Nelson

Photo credits: Cover, p. 1 Zdravinjo/Shutterstock.com; text frame Dmitry Natashin/ Shutterstock.com; caption boxes Azuzl/Shutterstock.com; background iulias/ Shutterstock.com; p. 5 Gwoeii/Shutterstock.com p. 7 Anneka/Shutterstock.com; p. 9 Captblack76/Shutterstock.com; p. 11 Nigel Pavitt/AWL Images/Getty Images; p. 13 Time & Life Pictures/The LIFE Picture Collection/Getty Images; p. 15 Ras67/ Wikimedia Commons; p. 17 Sylvie Bouchard/Shutterstock.com; p. 19 (both) Universal History Archive/Universal Images Group/Getty Images; p. 21 Hulton Archive/Hulton Archive/Getty Images; p. 23 Print Collector/Hulton Fine Art Collection/Getty Images; p. 25 Scewing/Wikimedia Commons; p. 27 (inset) Silver Screen Collection/Moviepix/Getty Images; p. 27 (main) Scott Barbour/Getty Images Entertainment/Getty Images; p. 29 7831/ Gamma-Rapho/Getty Images; p. 30 Saibarakova llona/Shutterstock.com.

Printed in the United States of America

CPSIA compliance information: Batch # CW16GS: For further information contact Gareth Stevens, New York, New York at 1-800-542-2595.

CONTENTS

THE LEGENDS

You might think witches ride broomsticks, cast spells, and have black cats. But there's a lot more to the witch **myth** than that. In fact, for hundreds of years, people were killed after being **accused** of witchcraft!

BEYOND THE MYTH

The scariest witch myths feature evil witches—but other stories from around the world have good witches in them!

Each **culture's** witch myths have a slightly different take on what witches can do and where they come from. Most say witches can control people or their surroundings using magic or other **supernatural** practices.

BEYOND THE MYTH

Witch myths came about as a way for people to explain evil or unusual things that happen in the world.

SUPERNATURAL!

In one group of witch myths, witches are born already having magical powers. In other stories, a witch chooses to learn magic, sometimes from a family member or another witch. This often includes studying how to cast spells!

BEYOND THE MYTH

Many European languages have old words that
mean sorcery, or magic, such as *sorcellerie* in French
and *stregoneria* in Italian.

9

Some African cultures believe groups of witches gathered to eat people! The Navajo told stories of witches who wore dead animal skins to become that animal. Christian myths said witches honored the devil. The Christian faith says that the devil is the source of all evil.

BEYOND THE MYTH

In Africa, it wasn't uncommon for a sick person to see a doctor *and* a witch doctor. Witch doctors were thought to free people from evil spells cast on them.

EARLY TALES

Homer's *The Odyssey* is the source of many monster myths—and it includes a witch! Circe lived on the island Aeaea and used magic to change sailors into animals. She turned the hero Odysseus's men into pigs!

BEYOND THE MYTH

Circe couldn't turn Odysseus into a pig because he'd
been given an herb by the gods to stop her.

Morgan Le Fay is a witch featured in many **versions** of the legend of King Arthur. Sometimes, she heals King Arthur. In other stories, Morgan Le Fay tries to get back at the queen for sending her away from the court.

BEYOND THE MYTH

The magical person most well known from the legend of King Arthur is the wizard Merlin. Some stories say he taught Morgan Le Fay her magic!

MORGAN LE FAY

15

English children who heard the story of Jenny Greenteeth had cause to fear witches! Sometimes called Wicked Jenny, this mythical witch was said to have supersharp teeth and green skin. She liked to eat children and old people!

BEYOND THE MYTH

The story of Jenny Greenteeth was likely used to keep English children from acting badly.

17

WITCH-HUNTS

Myths made people believe witches were real! From about the 14th century to the 18th century, towns in western Europe would "hunt" for witches. The hunts were often started when someone accused an enemy of witchcraft.

A Modeſt Enquiry
Into the Nature of
Witchcraft,
AND
How Perſons Guilty of that Crime
may be *Convicted* : And the means
uſed for their Diſcovery Diſcuſſed,
both *Negatively* and *Affirmatively,*
according to *SCRIPTURE* and
EXPERIENCE.

By John Hale,
Paſtor of the Church of Chriſt in Beverley,
Anno Domini. 1 6 9 7.

*When they ſay unto you, ſeek unto them that have
Familiar Spirits and unto Wizzards that peep,&c.
To the Law and to the Teſtimony ; if they ſpeak
not according to this word, it is becauſe there is no
light in them,* Iſaiah VIII. 19, 20.
That which I ſee not teach thou me, Job 34. 32.

BOSTON in N.E.
Printed by *B. Green,* and *J. Allen,* for
Benjamin Eliot under the Town Houſe. 1702.

BEYOND THE MYTH

Both men and women were accused of being witches.
Sometimes these people were healers, but more often,
they were just individuals others were angry with!

About three-fourths of European witch-hunts happened in France, northern Italy, western Germany, Switzerland, and nearby areas. About 110,000 people were put on trial for witchcraft, and between 40,000 and 60,000 were killed—many by being drowned or burned alive.

BEYOND THE MYTH

Being able to save yourself from drowning was a sure sign of being a witch! However, when tested, no one ever could. That means many innocent people died.

PLACING BLAME

The king and queen of Scotland started a witch-hunt in 1590 after a bad storm hit while they were aboard a ship. They blamed witches! They **tortured** about 70 people into saying they had done horrible things.

BEYOND THE MYTH

King James of Scotland was so interested in witchcraft, he wrote a book about it in 1597!

SALEM WITCH TRIALS

In 1692, a doctor in Salem, Massachusetts, said the illness of two young girls was caused by witchcraft! Other girls started to have similar "fits," which included a lot of screaming. The scared community accused more than 150 people of being witches.

BEYOND THE MYTH

Nineteen people were killed for being witches in Salem. Today, it's believed the first girls had eaten something that made them sick.

POPULAR WITCHES

In 1939, *The Wizard of Oz's* Wicked Witch of the West had a green face, black hat, and broomstick. This established the look of a witch in popular culture. The same look was used in the musical *Wicked* in 2003.

26

THE WIZARD OF OZ

WICKED

BEYOND THE MYTH

Witches' connection with broomsticks can be
traced back to Europe between the 14th century
and 17th century, like the witch trials.

Hermione Granger and Ginny Weasley might be the next most famous witches! These characters in the Harry Potter books and movies use their magical talents for good. In these stories, witches and wizards can choose to be good or evil!

BEYOND THE MYTH

Some myths say witches use animals in their magic. These animals are called familiars and are often pictured as black cats.

Witch Myths
Around the World

GREECE
Hectate is the Greek goddess of witchcraft and sorcery.

JAPAN
Okabe, or the cat witch, was an old woman who killed and ate young women.

CONGO
It was believed that the source of a witch's evil was found in her stomach.

THE UNITED STATES
The Bell Witch haunts a home in Tennessee. She's said to have poisoned the owner in 1817!

AUSTRALIA
Three sisters were turned to three stone mountains by a witch who wanted to keep them safe.

FOR MORE INFORMATION

BOOKS

Boyer, Crispin. *That's Creepy!* Washington, DC: National Geographic, 2013.

Landau, Elaine. *The Salem Witchcraft Trials: Would You Join the Madness?* Berkeley Heights, NJ: Enslow Elementary, 2014.

Netzley, Patricia. *Do Witches Exist?* San Diego, CA: ReferencePoint Press, Inc., 2016.

WEBSITES

The Salem Witch Trials

kids.nationalgeographic.com/kids/stories/history/salem-witch-trials/
Read more about the fear of witches that struck Salem, Massachusetts, in the 1600s.

Spooky Campfire Stories

americanfolklore.net/campfire.html
Find lots of scary stories to frighten your friends!

Publisher's note to educators and parents: Our editors have carefully reviewed these websites to ensure that they are suitable for students. Many Web sites change frequently, however, and we cannot guarantee that a site's future contents will continue to meet our high standards of quality and educational value. Be advised that students should be closely supervised whenever they access the Internet.

GLOSSARY

accuse: to blame

culture: the beliefs and ways of life of a group of people

myth: a legend or story

supernatural: unable to be explained or seeming to come from magic

torture: to cause someone pain to force them to do or say something

version: one form of something

INDEX